Roald Dahl
A Life of Imagination

by Jennifer Boothroyd

Lerner Publications Company • Minneapolis

Photo Acknowledgments

The photographs in this book are used with the permission of: © Rosie Tollemache, Courtesy of the Roald Dahl Museum and Story Centre, cover; © Bremner & Orr Design Consultants Ltd 1998, p. 4; © RDNL, Courtesy of the Roald Dahl Museum and Story Centre, pp. 6, 8, 9, 11, 12, 16, 17; © Hulton-Deutsch Collection/CORBIS, pp. 10, 22; © Disney Enterprises, Inc., Courtesy of the Roald Dahl Museum and Story Centre, p. 14; *The Gremlins* by Roald Dahl © Disney Enterprises, Inc. Used by permission of Random House, Inc. Image courtesy of the Los Angeles Public Library, 15; © Rex USA, p. 18; © Dave Hogan/Getty Images, p. 20; Kibea Publishing Company, p. 21; © Leonard McCombe/Time & Life Pictures/Getty Images, p. 24; © Sanjiro Minamikawa, Courtesy of the Roald Dahl Museum and Story Centre, p. 25; © Jan Baldwin, p. 26.

Text copyright © 2008 by Lerner Publishing Group, Inc.

All rights reserved. International copyright secured. No part of this book may be reproduced, stored in a retrieval system, or transmitted in any form or by any means—electronic, mechanical, photocopying, recording, or otherwise—without the prior written permission of Lerner Publishing Group, Inc., except for the inclusion of brief quotations in an acknowledged review.

Lerner Publications Company
A division of Lerner Publishing Group, Inc.
241 First Avenue North
Minneapolis, MN 55401 U.S.A.

Website address: www.lernerbooks.com

Words in **bold type** are explained in a glossary on page 31.

Library of Congress Cataloging-in-Publication Data

Boothroyd, Jennifer, 1972–
    Roald Dahl : a life of imagination / by Jennifer Boothroyd.
    p. cm. — (Pull ahead books : biographies)
    Includes index.
    ISBN-13: 978-0-8225-8825-2 (lib. bdg. : alk. paper)
    1. Dahl, Roald—Juvenile literature. 2. Authors, English—20th century—Biography—Juvenile literature. 3. Children's stories—Authorship—Juvenile literature. I. Title.
PR6054.A35Z52 2008
823'.914—dc22 [B]　　　　　　　　　　　　　　　　　　　　　　　　　2007019774

Manufactured in the United States of America
1 2 3 4 5 6 – JR – 13 12 11 10 09 08

Table of Contents

Have You Ever? 5

Growing Up 7

Becoming a Writer 13

A Children's Writer 19

Roald the Inventor 23

A Popular Imagination 27

Roald Dahl Timeline 28

More about Roald Dahl 30

Websites 30

Glossary 31

Index 32

Kids play inside a giant peach at the Roald Dahl Children's Gallery in Great Britain.

Have You Ever?

Have you ever lived inside a peach? Or flown through the air in a glass elevator? Roald Dahl did these things and more inside his head. He used his **imagination** to think of exciting ideas for stories. His imagination helped him become a famous author.

Three-year-old Roald with his mother, Sofie

Growing Up

Roald Dahl was born in Great Britain on September 13, 1916. Roald's mother liked to tell him bedtime stories. The stories were old fairy tales. Roald would imagine what the characters looked like.

When Roald was nine years old, he went to a **boarding school**. He did not like living away from home.

Roald lived at Saint Peter's School.

Roald and his three sisters

Roald missed his family. He wrote a letter home every week. Writing made him feel better.

Roald in his Royal Air Force uniform

After Roald finished school, he joined the Royal Air Force. His country was at war.

Roald became a **pilot**. Flying fighter planes was dangerous. Roald crashed twice.

Roald flew planes like these in the Royal Air Force.

The place was stiff with lorries of all sorts, and as we came down I could see the soldiers running about all over the place. I saw one stumble and pick himself up and go on running.

Shot Down Over Libya

"One of our planes is missing, but the pilot is safe," the communiqué said. Here is that pilot's report.

*The author of this factual report on Libyan air fighting is an RAF pilot at present in this country for medical reasons—*THE EDITORS.

THEY hung a label around my neck which said: "Flying Officer ——. Possible fractured skull base. Concussion and facial injuries. Church of England." I knew this because the medical orderly read the label out loud to me at the base hospital.

I tried to remember just why that label was there, and why it said these things. I tried to ask someone, but no one heard, so I gave it up and just lay still. Then slowly it all came back; not clearly and brightly at first, but a little dimly, as though by moonlight. In the end, I got it all.

Operational Order No. —— from Fighter H. Q. Western Desert to No. —— Squadron STOP Recco reports large number Italian vehicles parked close together 100 yards north of road 41 miles west of Sidi Barrani STOP Six Hurricanes attack at dusk.

The C.O. wandered in with it in his hand while we were having late tea in the mess tent, and handed it to Shorty, who was in charge of B Flight.

There was nothing unusual about the order—we had had similar ones every day for the last month— except, perhaps, that the job looked a little easier than most.

Shorty carefully extracted a fly from his tea and flicked it across the room. Then he read it a second time. "Hell's bells, what a piece of cake! Shall I take my flight, sir? We'll have to start right away."

He handed it to Oofy, who stopped picking the sand out of his starboard ear, read it slowly, then put it down and went on excavating his ear.

"I don't believe it," he said. "They never park them close together, but if they have, what a piece of cake!"

Outside, the Hurricanes were waiting, looking very dirty in their desert camouflage, which was just a coat of light-brown paint the color of sand. At a distance they merged into their surroundings. They looked a little thin and underfed, but very elegant.

Under the wings of each, in the shade, sat a fitter and rigger playing naughts and crosses in the hot sand, waiting to help start up.

"All clear."

"All clear, sir." I pressed the button; she coughed once or twice, as though clearing the sand from her throat, and started. Check the oxygen, check the petrol, brakes off, taxi into position behind Shorty, airscrew into fine pitch, mixture control to "rich," adjust tail trimmer; and now Shorty's holding his thumb up in the air. Yes, O.K., O.K. Thumb up, and everyone else does the same.

ILLUSTRATED BY JOHN F. GOULD

Six dusty left arms went out, six throttles were gently pushed forward and the six machines moved away, churning up the dust with their airscrews and creating a minor sandstorm in their wake. Six people began to concentrate.

Shorty swung a bit to the right on take-off, but he always did that, and we all knew he always did it, so it didn't matter. Once air-borne, undercart up, adjust the revs, regulate the mixture and start looking.

This business of looking is the most important part of a fighter-pilot's job. You've got to have a rubber neck and you've got to keep it moving the whole time from the moment you get into the air to the moment you arrive back at your base. If you don't, you won't last long. You turn slowly from the extreme left to the extreme right, glancing at your instruments as you go past; and then, looking up high, you turn back again from right to left to start all over again.

Don't start gazing into your cockpit, or sure as eggs, you'll get jumped sooner or later; and don't start daydreaming or looking at the beautiful scenery—there's no future in it.

And so we, too, started looking. We were flying straight into the sun, which was just beginning to touch the horizon. It looked like a blood orange. Shorty was leading, with two of us close in on either side in v formation, with Oofy weaving about in the rear, watching our tails. I was on the starboard side, next to Shorty, and his wing tip was only about twelve feet away. *(Continued on Page 38)*

Roald's plane crash story was in the *Saturday Evening Post* in 1942.

Becoming a Writer

Roald wrote about one of his plane crashes. A magazine printed his story. Roald also wrote a **fantasy** story. It was about little monsters that make planes crash.

Walt Disney liked Roald's monster story. He wanted to make it into a movie.

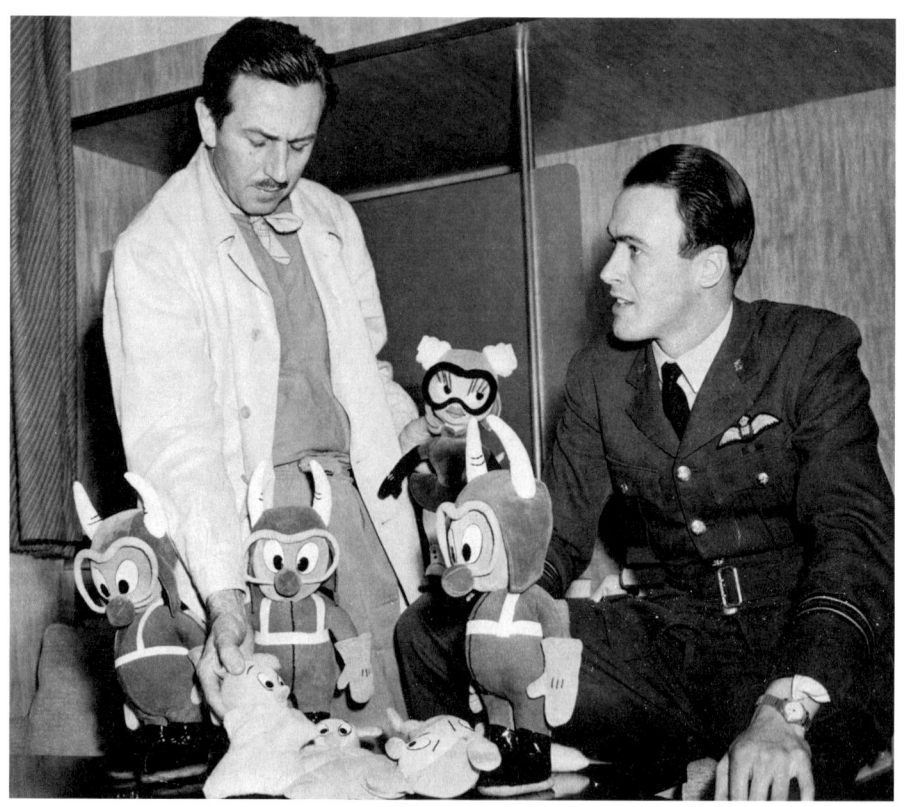

Walt Disney, on the left, with Roald and toy monsters

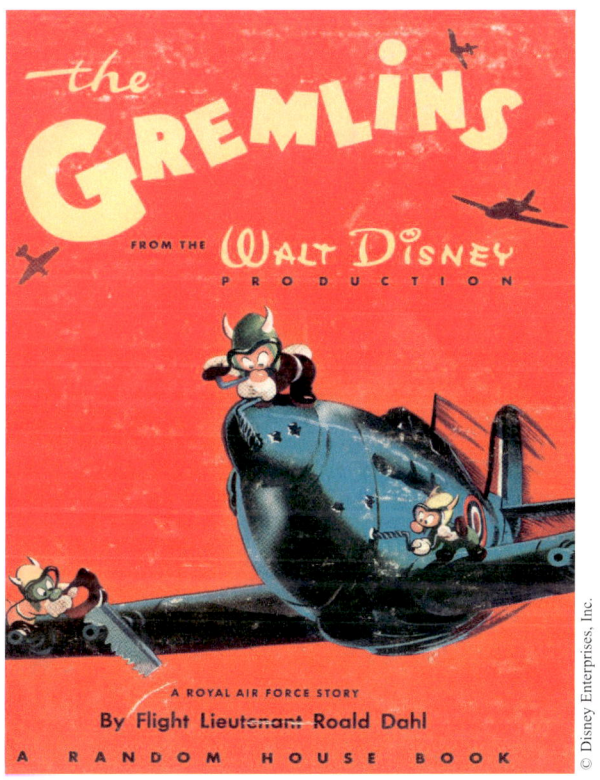

Roald's monster story was called *The Gremlins*.

Walt changed his mind. He turned the story into a picture book instead.

Roald was always thinking of new story ideas. He wrote his thoughts in a notebook.

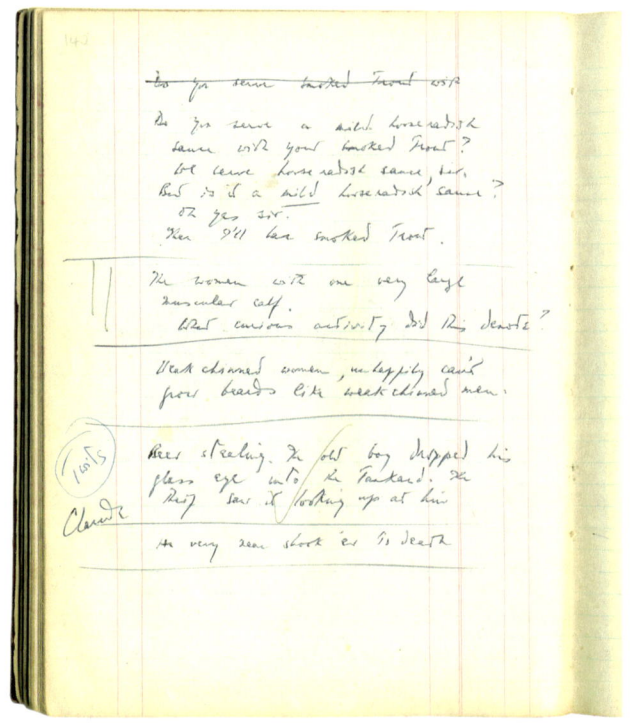

A page from Roald's notebook

Roald's writing hut

Roald built a small hut in his yard. This is where he wrote his stories. He filled the hut with things to help his imagination.

Roald with his wife and children in 1970

A Children's Writer

Roald got married and became a father. He used his imagination to make up stories for his children. Roald decided to make these stories into books. The first story became the book *James and the Giant Peach*.

For his next book, Roald imagined a fantastic candy factory.

The factory in Roald's book made all kinds of sweets.

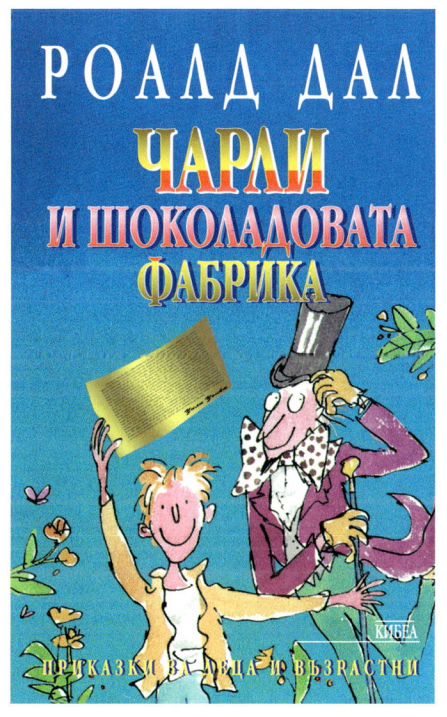

Charlie and the Chocolate Factory in Bulgarian

This book, *Charlie and the Chocolate Factory,* became very **popular**. Children all over the world read it.

Roald and his son, Theo

Roald the Inventor

Roald used his imagination for more than writing stories. He also invented things. Roald's son hurt his head in an accident. Roald imagined a tool that could help heal the **injury**.

Roald worked with a doctor and a friend to create the tool. It helped thousands of children get better.

Stanley Wade, Roald's friend, holds the tool they invented.

Roald enjoyed gardening both indoors and outside.

Roald also invented kites, puzzle games, and garden tools.

Roald works in his writing hut.

A Popular Imagination

Roald Dahl died in 1990. He had written more than twenty children's books. Roald's imagination helped him become one of the most popular authors in the world.

ROALD DAHL TIMELINE

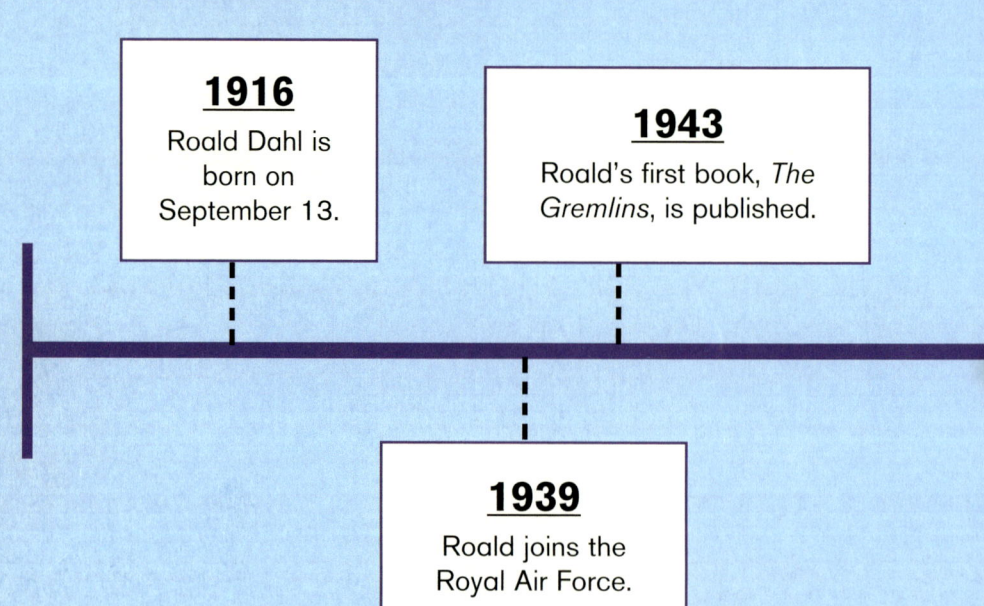

1916
Roald Dahl is born on September 13.

1943
Roald's first book, *The Gremlins*, is published.

1939
Roald joins the Royal Air Force.

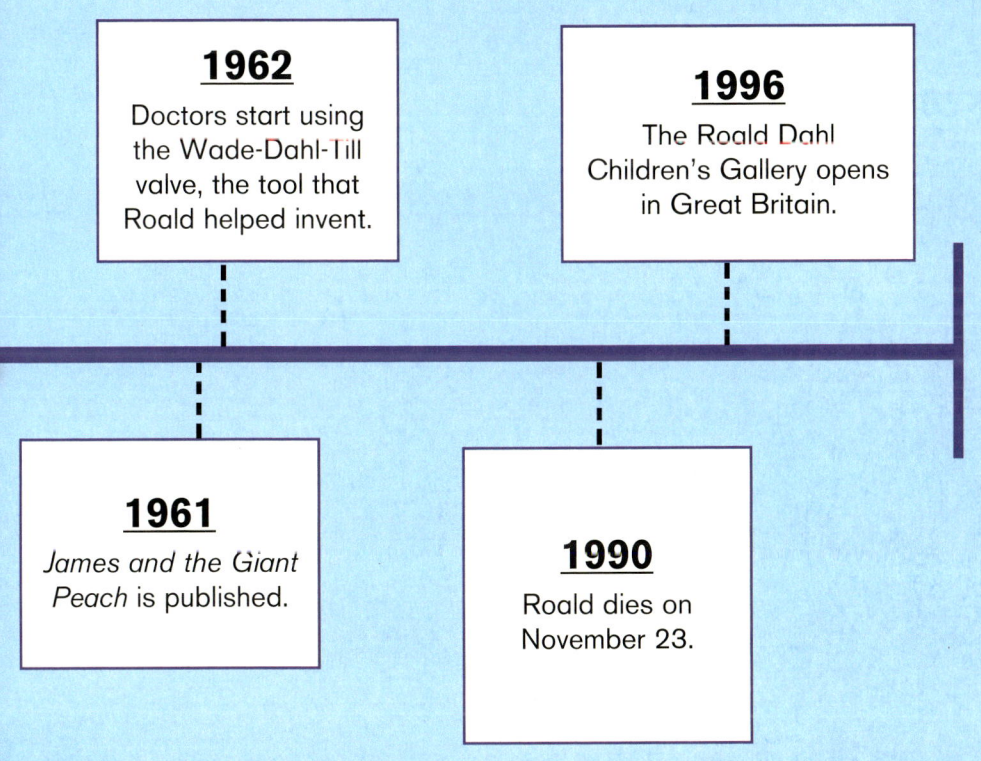

More about Roald Dahl

- Roald's daughter Olivia became sick and died when she was seven years old. Roald dedicated his book *The BFG* to her.

- One of the schools Roald went to was close to a large candy company. When a new candy was invented, the company let the students try it to see if they liked it or not.

- After Roald finished writing *Charlie and the Chocolate Factory*, he let his nephew, Nicholas, read it. Nicholas told Uncle Roald that it was boring. So Roald rewrote the story to make it more interesting.

Websites

Roald Dahl
http://www.roalddahl.com

Roald Dahl Children's Gallery
http://www.buckscc.gov.uk/bcc/content/index.jsp?contentid=-1191581755

Roald Dahl Museum and Story Centre
http://www.roalddahlmuseum.org

Glossary

boarding school: a school where students live and go to school

fantasy: make-believe

imagination: ability to think about things creatively or in a new way

injury: harm or damage to a body part

pilot: a person who flies an airplane

popular: well liked

Index

bedtime stories, 7
birth, 7, 28

Charlie and the Chocolate Factory, 21, 30

death, 27, 29
Disney, Walt, 14

flying, 11

Great Britain, 4, 7, 29
Gremlins, The, 28

inventions, 23, 24, 25, 29

James and the Giant Peach, 19, 28

Roald Dahl Children's Gallery, 4, 29
Royal Air Force, 11, 28

school, 8, 30

Wade, Stanley, 24
Wade-Dahl-Till valve, 23, 24, 29
writing, 9, 13, 16, 17